Don't Be a HO HO HO
for
Valentine's Day!

The only thing getting popped should be the champagne cork.

THE MANIFESTO

Don't be a **HO HO HO** this Valentine's Day,
I've wiped too many tears from hoes who gave it away.

You rewarded him nothing and hoped he would grow,
That's not romance, sweetheart — that's a pattern you know.

This book ends the begging, the waiting, the plea,
So sit down and listen to an old lady like me.

Men love the Valentine's HO — she never says no.
No flowers, no dinner — she still puts on a show.

NO DATE THIS YEAR

No Valentine this year? Don't look so upset.
You haven't learned the lessons from being a ho yet.

After years of rewarding nothing — time to reward you,
Time to reflect instead of giving some loser a screw.

Being alone isn't tragic, it's actually great,
Read about being a lady and how to properly date.

Men love the Valentine's HO — she never says no.
No flowers, no dinner — she still puts on a show.

THE "I DON'T DO VALENTINE'S" GUY

He said Valentine's Day was fake and a scam,
A very convenient rule for a cheap, lazy man.

You said he was deep, not into that stuff,
Funny how "deep" always means doing nothing is enough.

Men don't skip Valentine's with women they love,
They roll out the red carpet, beyond and above.

Men love the Valentine's ho — she's easy to please.
No plans, no gift — just gets on her knees.

LOW MAINTENANCE

You bragged you were low maintenance, "I'm easy, I'm cool,"
He heard that loud and clear — congratulations, fool.

You said, "I'm not like those other girls who need a lot,"
You just take what you get so you don't stir the pot.

Men don't respect fear dressed up as being nice,
If you're scared to require, you're paying the price.

Men love the Valentine's ho — she's basically free.
No pearls, no card — still bursting with glee.

Low Maintenance = Low Value.

THE BARE-MINIMUM GUY

Came over at 11 p.m. and then tried to get some,
That means he was horny and thinks you are dumb.

You said, "At least he came over, I know it was late."
Wake up — he took a respectable girl on a Valentine's date.

The bare minimum is never okay,
Especially not on Valentine's Day.
You don't love yourself — there is no fucking way!

Men love the Valentine's HO — she never says no.
No flowers, no dinner — she still puts on a show.

THE "WE DON'T NEED LABELS" GUY

Not girlfriend, not partner, not favorite boo,
If you don't get a label, he's using you.

You said, "We don't need a label, he thinks labels are lame,"
If he liked you, sweetheart, he wouldn't feel the same.

No label means this, and it's painfully clear:
He'll fuck you on Valentine's Day, but you won't be here next year.

Men love the Valentine's ho — she dresses too tight.
No gift, no message — still stays the night.

THE "WHAT DO YOU WANT TO DO?" GUY

He came over and said, "So... what do you want to do?"
It's Valentine's Day — he didn't think this through.

"But he worked all day, he's got so much on his mind,"
You make Olympic-level excuses for a man who's unkind.

In my day, men knew how to protect and provide,
Not act like pussy boys who can't decide.

Men love the Valentine's HO — she never says no.
No flowers, no dinner — she still puts on a show.

THE 7-ELEVEN VALENTINE

He showed up with roses from 7-Eleven,
Chocolate half-melted — very romantic at seven.

You said, "At least he tried, it's sweet in a way—"
Sweet? He bought this ten minutes ago on Valentine's Day.

Men who care plan ahead, they don't grab and run,
A 7-Eleven Valentine means you weren't the one.

Men love the Valentine's ho — she never says no.
No flowers, no dinner — she still puts on a show.

THE "WE'LL DO IT ANOTHER DAY" GUY

He said, "Valentine's is crazy, let's do another day,"
Funny how "another day" means you're not the play.

You said, "He's thoughtful, he's sweet, he's okay—"
STOP! None of that showed up Valentine's Day.

Men know Valentine's is important to a lady,
If he's not making plans, he's doing something shady.

Men love the Valentine's ho — she never says no.
No flowers, no dinner — she still puts on a show.

SITUATIONSHIP GUY

He said, "You're a cool girl, let's situationship.
We're progressive in 2026 — there is no relationship."

You said, "That's cool, we can explore."
That attitude is exactly what men don't adore!

Men will never have to think things through
If they care about another man screwing you.

Men love the Valentine's ho — she never says no.
No flowers, no dinner — she still puts on a show.

GRANDMA INTERRUPTS

Different name, same man, just swap out the face,
Same excuses, same ending, same damn place.

You say, "This one feels different," every damn year,
Funny how "different" always disappears.

Insanity is this — and I'll say it slow:
Doing the same shit and acting shocked by the blow.

Men love the Valentine's ho — she plays with his thing.
No card, no dinner — still treats him like a king.

"YOU'RE DIFFERENT"

He said, "You're different — how cliché,"
He'll say anything just to get a lay.

You said, "But I like him, I think it's true,"
Really — are you going on 12 or 32?

If you weren't different than the rest,
Flowers, candy, and a diamond would be his best.

Men love the Valentine's ho — she's insecure.
No card, no text — but will act like a Wh*re.

SEX FIRST

You slept with him on the first date,
Now you wonder why you're treated second-rate.

You said, "No, he liked me, I could tell,"
So did the prostitute taking payments through Zelle.

Good guys want to know who you are,
Bad guys don't give a shit — they've got a low bar.

Men love the Valentine's ho — she's insecure.
No card, no text — but will act like a Wh*re.

"I DON'T NEED GIFTS"

Women were told not to take what a man can,
That advice came from ugly women or an ugly man.

Beta men want a mommy, a girl to provide,
An alpha wants a feminine woman by his side.

He needs to spend money — can't you see?
Men don't respect anything easy or free.

Men love the Valentine's ho — she's easy to please.
No plans, no gift — just gets on her knees.

I told him I don't need gifts.
Men don't respect free.
That's why you get treated like shit.
Men spend money on women they LIKE.
Even I know that.

THE VALENTINE'S DAY RULE

He said, "It's just a day, it doesn't mean a thing,"
Funny how that day shows effort — or the lack of it — clear as spring.

You said, "He cares, he just doesn't show it that way,"
Valentine's Day is exactly how men show where you stay.

No dinner, no flowers, no gift to pursue?
Then no sex, no tears, no confusion for you.

Men love the Valentine's ho — she never says no.
No flowers, no dinner — she still puts on a show.

HE DOESN'T LIKE YOU

He takes days to text, won't plan, won't decide,
You're convenient for now — not girlfriend on his side.

You say, "He's busy, he's stressed, he's got so much to do,"
Funny how he's never too busy for women he wants to pursue.

Men don't act unsure with women they choose,
If you're still confused, that is the news.

Men love the Valentine's ho — she's good to go.
No candy, no diamonds — still performs like a pro.

STAY SINGLE

You're scared of being single like that's the disgrace,
But begging for crumbs is the real ugly place.

You say, "I'm so lonely, I could die,"
Then stop picking the wrong fucking guy.

Single is calm, it's dignity, peace,
Staying for nothing is where standards decrease.

Men love the Valentine's ho — she never says no.
No flowers, no dinner — she still puts on a show.

WHY ARE YOU WITH YOUR FRIENDS?

You praise this man like he's perfect and great,
Funny how no one you know has met him to date.

You cry all the time, say, "He hates Valentine's Day,"
So why are you out with your friends anyway?

If he wanted to claim you, make plans, or be seen,
You wouldn't be crying — you'd be his Valentine queen.

Men love the Valentine's ho — she never says no.
No flowers, no dinner — she still puts on a show.

BACK IN MY DAY

Back in my day, men courted with time,
They showed up first — that was the sign.

Now you slut your way through with nothing to show,
You repeat it, blame men — like you don't know.

Men want what they earn, not what's handed for free,
Smart women move slower — they let men be.

Men love the Valentine's ho — she's easy to please.
No plans, no gift — just gets on her knees.

ENGRAVE IT IN STONE!

No Valentine's gift?
Stay alone.

No date, no plan, nothing to show?
Then close the door tight and say no to the no.

If women required standards, we'd all have a ring.
No standards are exactly why there's ghosting.

So yes — men love the Valentine's ho.
Her self-worth is low.
No flowers, no dinner — she still puts on a show.

But you?
You LOVE yourself too much for that.
Listen to grandma, dear.

www.ingramcontent.com/pod-product-compliance
Lightning Source LLC
Chambersburg PA
CBHW060857270326
41934CB00003B/173

9781971419084